KACHINAS

A SELECTED BIBLIOGRAPHY

AVACHOYA

Spotted or speckled corn kachina. Meant to represent the different
varieties of corn.

KACHINAS
A SELECTED BIBLIOGRAPHY

Marcia Muth

Illustrations by Glen Strock

Sunstone Press
Santa Fe, New Mexico

For

Judi Armstrong

FIRST EDITION
Printed in the United States of America

Library of Congress Cataloging in Publication Data:

Muth, Marcia, 1919-
    Kachinas: a selected bibliography.

1. Katcinas—Bibliography. 2. Hopi Indians— Religion and mythology—Bibliography.
3. Indians of North America—Southwest, New Religion and mythology—Bibliography. I. Title.
Z1210.H6M87   1983   (E99.H7) 016.745592-'21'08997   83–18302
ISBN: 0-86534-031-5

Published in 1984 by Sunstone Press   Post Office Box 2321   Santa Fe, New Mexico 87504-2321   USA

TABLE OF CONTENTS

FOREWORD

Like many residents and visitors in the Southwest, I have been fascinated by kachinas. They combine the artistic with the mystic, touching something elemental in each one of us. Collecting or even simply admiring kachinas in shops or museums is only part of the story. The second part is reading and studying about them; thus, this book came into being. It is not intended to be an exhaustive list but a selected one. And, because illustrations of kachinas are so important, they have been noted. I have also indicated, whenever possible, whether the illustrations are in color or black & white.

AHÖLA
A chief kachina associated with growth and reproduction.

INTRODUCTION

The word *kachina* has an exotic sound, particularly to those who are not inhabitants of the Southwestern United States. The sound of the word has a harshness, a sound of force and magic. This is fitting since kachinas are supposed to have both power and magic — at least in legend.

Spellings of the word vary and, while *kachina* is the most familiar and most popular, the more official form is *katsina*. Thus, if you go to a library and look for material on kachinas you will be referred to the latter spelling. In various books you can also find references to *cachina*, *kacina*, *katzina* and several other variations. All this is caused by the fact that the Indians had no written language and interpreters followed their individual preferences when recording Indian words.

Probably the most important thing to remember about kachinas is that they are more than the wooden figures offered for sale in stores and at Indian markets. These are indeed "doll figures" but the person interested in collecting them should also make an effort to understand the kachina mythology and its meaning.

Hopi Indian religion is a pantheistic and ritualistic religion. In that sense the word kachina can be used in three different ways. Paramount, of course, is the reference to the supernatural spirits or beings. You might call these the "original" kachinas. But the word also refers to the dancers who assume the masks and costumes of those spirit beings. They become the living impersonators of the legends much in the same way that Christians perform the Passion Play or act out the early miracle plays. Finally, kachinas may mean the painted wooden dolls. These dolls range from the simplest forms with a few primary colors to elaborate figures with paint, feathers, fur and cloth. In size they may range from an inch to two or three feet. As tourists and collectors have learned, the miniature kachinas and the largest ones command the greatest prices.

Originally the kachina doll was devised as a teaching device. Children were given the dolls as part of their religious training.

9

They were given to the children to help them learn the different kachinas, their characteristics, names and duties. This is still done but now they have also become an important source of income to Indian artisans.

While all the Pueblos use kachinas to some extent, they are predominant among the Hopi and Zuni Indians. It has been estimated that there are at least 250 Hopi kachinas, each with its own function and mythology.

Who then are the kachinas? They were, according to legend, supernatural beings who at one time lived with the people. But when familiarity began to breed indifference and disrespect, the kachinas left. However, because they were superior beings and had a sense of responsibility toward the people whom they had tried to help, they did not leave them without the promise of hope and help. Before the kachinas left, so the legend goes, they taught the people the necessary rituals so that the spirits could still be contacted. In addition to the rituals, the kachinas taught a favored few how to make the masks and costumes needed to impersonate the actual kachinas once they were gone.

The relationship between the kachinas and their people was one familiar to all such cooperative ventures. The kachinas had performed valuable services. They were the lords of the earth but they were kindly. They brought gifts, they danced, they understood the special sadness and loneliness that humans suffer. According to legend, they taught people all kinds of things from hunting to the making of tools and other artifacts. One of their most important functions in this arid land was to bring rain when it was needed. However, for whatever reasons, the kachinas left, never to return in person.

The time of the kachinas is past, but their legend remains. Two modern interpretations come to mind — one, that kachinas are a variation on the lost paradise or Eden theme. However, Indian people are not dismissed from the sacred land but, because of their conduct, the gods themselves withdrew and the people were henceforth separated physically from the supernatural. True, the gods had left behind ritual, prayers and directions, but from then on the people had to work for what they wanted, whether rain, fertile crops or other needs.

In a technological space-oriented age, there is another possible interpretation of the kachinas. Were these benign presences from another galaxy? Could they have been superior beings trying to advance the civilization they found on earth? Hopi myths, when examined in this light, certainly support such a concept — as do myths of the Navajo, Zuni and other tribes.

Whatever you believe the kachinas to have been — or even if you question their existence at all — the visible remains of the legends are the kachina dancers and the kachina dolls.

It is believed that the person who dons the mask and the costume of a kachina becomes temporarily imbued with the actual spirit and qualities of that particular kachina. However, they are not looked upon as gods but only as symbols of the gods.

Feminism has no part in the kachina dances. Only men take part and they represent male and female kachinas.

The dancers' functions are varied. They dance for rain, for the spiritual good of the community and for any specific needs. Some kachinas are believed to have the power to cure certain diseases. Each kachina has a defined function and is believed to be the spirit of an animal, bird, insect, plant, place, object or person.

Clowns, such as the Koshares, are a popular form of kachina. They often serve a dual function. In the midst of all the solemnity, the clowns offer relief from tension. They are entertainers and mimics. A second function is to impose a form of community censure by ridiculing any individual who has misbehaved during the year. The antics of the clowns are sometimes ribald and occasionally they make fun of the Anglos watching their dances.

The season or time of the kachinas starts with the winter solstice and ends in mid or late July. It is said that the Hopi kachinas live on the San Francisco peaks near Flagstaff, Arizona and that they come down to visit during those few months.

The pantheon of kachinas is not fixed. A kachina may disappear, a new kachina be added — much in the way the calendar of saints was rearranged a few years ago.

Since it is believed that the influence of the kachinas extends beyond the pueblos, how much, perhaps, do we all owe to the portrayers, to the dances? It might be well to remember too, that while most of the kachinas are kind and filled with benevolence, there are a few ogre kachinas whose purpose is to pursue and rebuke evildoers.

Kachina dolls used to be available only at trading posts or from Indians at the Pueblos or on the reservations, but now they can be found in any shop that carries Indian goods. The early collectors of kachina dolls were government agents who were among the first to come into contact with the Indians. At that time the Indians, especially the Hopi, did not want to sell kachina dolls but the new intruders were persistent and demanding. In time as the Indian world shrank through contact with the wider world and a greater interest in Indian crafts developed, the Hopi as well as other Indians began to sell kachinas to augment their incomes.

Kachina dolls are usually made of cottonwood. The early kachinas were painted with natural paints and were rigid in shape. But, because of the demand for the kachinas by outsiders, changes have come about in the making of them. For example, commercial paints are now generally used and the dolls are often shown in "action" poses. Where live evergreen was once used, now green yarn or plastic greenery is used or in some cases the wood is simply carved and painted to represent the greenery. Noses, arms and so forth are glued on rather than pegged into place.

Since the feathers of certain birds can no longer be legally used, feathers from such commonplace creatures as chickens are substituted or carved feathers have also become common practice.

After World War II there was a steadily increasing demand for Indian crafts of all kinds. Along with this there developed an avid interest in the individual Indian craftsman. Although it was contrary to tribal customs, some Hopis began to sign their kachinas and became well-known to collectors who bought their work as soon as it was available. The ever-increasing sales after 1960 resulted in more realistic carving, more elaborate costumes, striking action poses and, of course, higher prices. More craftsmen became known for their work and despite the tradition of "men only," women began to carve the dolls also. Today, many miniature kachinas are made by women.

In buying kachinas, it is best to know the seller's reputation and sense of integrity. There are kachinas turned out by machine lathe. Although such dolls cannot legally be sold as genuine kachinas, there is often a policy of "buyer beware." Examine any kachina carefully for signs of individual carving. The feet, for example, should be carved not just indicated as a split in the wood. Complete symmetry in a figure should be regarded with some suspicion.

There are now an infinite variety of kachinas available. The choices have considerable range in details: sizes, costumes, poses and uniqueness.

Collecting kachinas can be most rewarding, aesthetically and intellectually. These are not "dolls" in our traditional sense but mythological figures with roots in a civilization and culture which was active long before Christopher Columbus sighted land. As living history, kachinas proudly attest to being larger than life legends, legends that do not die as long as there are people willing to recreate them in story and song, picture and dance.

Santa Fe, New Mexico, 1983

EOTOTO

The chief of all the kachinas. It is he who controls the seasons and has knowledge of all the ceremonies.

A

Arizona Highways. "Arizona Highways presents a treasury of Arizona's colorful Indians." Phoenix, AZ: © 1967. Unnumbered. Two pages of color illustrations.

Arizona Highways. "Living spirits of kachinas." Phoenix, AZ: June 1971: 47:6, 48 pp. Black & white and color illustrations; front & back covers.

B

Bahti, Tom. An introduction to Southwestern Indian arts & crafts. Las Vegas, NE: KC Publications, © 1966, pp. 18, 20-22. Black & white and color illustrations.

_____. Southwestern Indian ceremonials. Las Vegas, NE: KC Publications, © 1970, pp. 24, 29, 35, 39. Black & white and color illustrations.

Bischoff, Kay. Kachina dolls, cut and color. (Revised text.) Drawings by Eugene H. Bischoff. Albuquerque, NM: Eukabi Publishers, © 1952, unnumbered. Black & white illustrations.

Boelter, Homer H. Portfolio of Hopi kachinas. Hollywood, CA: H.H. Boelter Lithography (1969), 2 v. Vol 2 = color plates.

Breunig, Robert. Kachina Dolls. Flagstaff, AZ: Museum of Northern Arizona, 1983, 32 pp. Black & white and color illustrations.

Bunzel, Ruth L. Zuni katcinas; an analytical study. Forty-seventh annual report of the Bureau of American Ethnology to the Secretary of the Smithsonian Institution, 1929-30. Washington, DC: 1932, pp. 837-1086. Black & white and color illustrations.

_____. *Zuni katcinas; an analytical study.* Reprint of Bureau of American Ethnology report. Glorieta, NM: Rio Grande Press, © 1973, 1108 pp. Black & white and color illustrations.

_____. *Zuni katcinas.* Extract from the forty-seventh annual report of the Bureau of American Ethnology. Washington, DC: US Gov't Print. Off., 1932, 249 pp. Black & white and color illustrations.

C

Chiara, Joan. "Kachina dolls." *Hobbies*, V. 82, Dec. 1977, p. 38. Illustrations.

Cody, Bertha, P. "Kachina dolls." *The Masterkey*, V. 13, 1939, Los Angeles.

Colton, Harold S. *Hopi kachina dolls with a key to their identification.* Albuquerque: University of New Mexico Press, © 1949, 144 pp. Black & white and color illustrations.

_____. _____. Rev. ed. 1959, 150 pp. Reprinted 1979. Black & white and color illustrations.

_____. "Kachina dolls." *Arizona Highways*, 26:8 July 1950, pp. 8-13. Black & white and color illustrations; front cover.

_____. "What is a katchina?" *Plateau.*

Conkling, Christopher. "The Kachina spirits." *Artists of the Sun* Supplement to the *Santa Fe Reporter*, August 17, 1983, pp. 61-63. Black & white illustrations.

Cosner, Shaaron. "Kachina dolls; carved from cottonwood root, Hopi religious figures can be difficult to decipher but rewarding to collect." *Americana*, Sept. 1976, pp. 26-29. Illustrations.

Coze, Paul. "Kachinas: masked dancers of the Southwest." *National Geographic Magazine,* 112:2, August 1957, pp. 219 -236. Black & white and color illustrations.

_____. "Of clowns and mudheads." *Arizona Highways,* 28:8, August, 1952, pp. 18-29. Black & white and color illustrations.

Custer, Augusta H. "Zuni katchinas." *School Arts Magazine,* 33:1, Sept. 1933, pp. 35-38. Black & white illustrations.

D

DeHuff, Elizabeth Willis. *Five little katchinas.* Illustrations by Fred Kabotie. Boston: Houghton Mifflin, 1930, 86 pp. Color illustrations.

Day-ga-khle-chee. See: Millett, Clair A.

Dockstader, Frederick J. "Indian art in the Southwest." In *American Indian art, form and tradition.* An exhibition organized by: Walker Art Center Indian Art Association, the Minneapolis Institute of the Arts. New York: Dutton, 1972, pp. 62-69. Black & white and color illustrations.

_____. *The kachina and the white man; a study of the influences of white culture on the Hopi Kachina cult.* Cranbrook: Institute of Science Bulletin 35, 1954, 185 pp. Black & white and color illustrations. Another version was published as the author's dissertation (Western Reserve University) with the title *White influence on the Hopi kachina cult.*

Dodge, Natt N., and Zim, Herbert S. *The Southwest, a guide to the wide open spaces.* New York: Golden Press © 1955, 160 pp., pp. 30-31. Color illustrations including title page.

Douglas, Frederic H., and D'Hanoncourt, Rene. *Indian art of the United States.* New York: The Museum of Modern Art, © 1941, 219 pp., p. 127. Black & white illustrations.

Dutton, Bertha P. *Indian artistry in wood and other media.* Santa Fe, NM: School of American Research Papers, New Series, No. 47, 1957, 28pp. Black & white illustrations, color cover.

_____. *Indians of the American Southwest.* Englewood Cliffs, NJ: Prentice-Hall, © 1975, pp. 44-61, 258-60. Black & white illustrations, fig. 12.

_____. "Katsina figures." In her *Indians of the Southwest, pocket handbook.* Santa Fe, NM: Southwestern Association on Indian Affairs, Inc., 1963, pp. 112-114. Black & white illustrations, front & back color covers.

Dutton, Bertha, and Olin, Caroline. *Myths & legends of the Indians of the southwest; Hopi, Acoma, Tewa, Zuni.* Santa Barbara, CA: Bellerophon Books, © 1978, unnumbered. Black & white illustrations.

E

Earle, Edwin, and Kennard, Edward A. *Hopi kachinas.* New York: J.J. Augustin, 1938, 40pp. Color illustrations.

_____. _____. 2nd ed., revised. New York: Museum of the American Indian, Heye Foundation, 1971, 50 pp. Color illustrations.

_____. *A portfolio of 28 plates in full color from the book Hopi kachinas.* New York: Museum of the American Indian, 1971. 28 plates. Color illustrations.

Ellis, Florence H. "A pantheon of kachinas." *The Indian arts of New Mexico.* Santa Fe: *New Mexico Magazine,* © 1975, unnumbered. Black & white and color illustrations.

_____. _____. *New Mexico Magazine,* 53:3, March 1975, pp. 13-18. *Black & white and color illustrations. front & back color covers.*

KWEO

Wolf kachina. Usually accompanies the deer kachina in dances.
Believed to be an aid to hunters.

The Encyclopedia Americana. International ed. New York: © 1977. Vol. 9, p. 255, black & white illustrations; vol. 14, p. 370; vol. 15, p. 25, black & white illustrations; vol. 22, p. 776, color illustrations.

Encyclopaedia Britannica. Chicago: 1967. Vol 7, p. 558, plate III, color illustration; vol. 18 (primitive art), plate IV, color illustration.

Encyclopedia of World Art. New York: McGraw Hill, © 1962. Vol. 6, col. 7; vol. 10, cols. 705, 706; plate 351. Black & white illustration.

Erickson, Jon T. *Kachinas, an evolving Hopi art form?* Phoenix, AZ: Heard Museum, © 1977, 112 pp. Black & white illustrations.

Evanoff, Betty. "Kachina dolls." *Antiques Journal* 36, May 1981, pp. 20-22. Illustrations.

F

Feder, Norman. *American Indian art*. New York: Abrams: 1969, pp. 79-86. Black & white illustrations.

Feest, Christian F. *Native arts of North America*. New York: Oxford University Press, 1980, pp. 164, 183-85. Black & white and color illustrations.

Fewkes, Jesse W. *Dolls of the Tusayan Indians*. Leiden: International Archiv für Ethnologie, 1894, vol. 2, pp. 45-73. Color illustrations.

_____. *Hopi katchinas, drawn by native artists*. Twentieth annual report of the Bureau of American Ethnology, 1899-1900. Washington, DC: 19034, pp. 3-126. Color illustrations.

_____. _____. Reprint. Chicago: Rio Grande Press, 1962, 190 pp. Color illustrations.

_____. "An interpretation of katcina worship." *Journal of American Folklore* 14, 1901, pp. 81-84.

_____. "Sky-God personations in Hopi worship." *Journal of American Folklore*, 15, 1902, pp. 14-32. Illustrations.

_____. *Tusayan kachinas.* Fifteenth annual report of the Bureau of American Ethnology. Washington, DC: 1897, pp. 245-313. Black & white and color illustrations.

G

Greenlee, Donna. *The kachina doll book.* Scottsdale, AZ: Fun Publishing Co., 1972, 32 pp. Black & white illustrations.

_____. *The kachina doll book 2.* Scottsdale, AZ: Fun Publishing Co., 1973, 32 pp. Black & white illustrations.

_____. *Kachina doll coloring book.* Scottsdale, AZ: (Fun Publishing Co., 1976?), 30 pp. Black & white Illustrations.

H

Hall, J.R. "Southwestern kachinas." *Hobbies* 62, August 1957, p. 48. Illustrations.

Heard Museum of Anthropology and Primitive Art. *Dancing Kachinas: a Hopi artist's documentary.* Original paintings by Cliff Bahnimptewa. Phoenix: 1971, unnumbered. Color illustrations.

Hodge, Gene Meany. *The kachinas are coming; Pueblo Indian kachina dolls with related folktales.* Los Angeles: Stellar-Miller Co., 1938, 129 pp. Color illustrations.

_____. _____. Reprint. Flagstaff, AZ: Northland Press, 1967, 129 pp. Color illustrations.

Holien, Elaine Baran. "Kachinas." *El Palacio* 76:4, 1970, pp. 1-15. Black & white illustrations.

Holstein, Philip M., and Erdman, Donnelley. *Enduring visions, 1000 years of southwestern Indian art.* Aspen, CO: The Aspen Center for the Visual Arts, 1979, pp. 9, 11-16. Color illustrations; front cover.

Hough, Walter. *The Hopi Indian collection in the U.S. National Museum.* Washington, DC: Gov't Print. Off., 1918. Reprint of the Proceedings, U.S. National Museum, no. 2235, vol. 54, pp. 235-96. Illustrations.

Hunt, Walter B. *Kachina dolls.* Milwaukee: Milwaukee Public Museum, 1958. Unnumbered. "Popular science handbook series, no. 7, Sept. 1957. Black & white and color illustrations.

J

James, Harry C. *The Hopi Indians, their history and their culture.* Caldwell Idaho: Caxton, 1956, pp. 169-173. Black & white illustrations.

Johnston, Bernice. *Speaking of Indians, with an accent on the Southwest.* Tucson AZ: University of Arizona Press, © 1970, pp. 78-79, 86-87. Black & white illustrations.

K

Kabotie, Fred. "Hopi kachina." *Newark Museum Quarterly,* 28, Spring 1977, p. 23. Illustration only.

KWIKWILYAGA

This kachina is an imitator, mocking the actions of the other kachinas and sometimes those of spectators.

Kabotie, Fred, and Belknap, Bill. *Fred Kabotie: Hopi Indian Artist an autobiography told with Bill Belknap.* Flagstaff, AZ: Museum of Northern Arizona, Northland Press, 1977, 149 pp. Black & white and color illustrations.

Kennedy, Paul E. *North American Indian design coloring book.* New York: Dover, © 1971. Unnumbered. Black & white illustrations.

Koenig, Seymour, and Koenig, Harriet. *Hopi clay. Hopi ceremony, an exhibition of Hopi art.* Katonah, NY: The Katonah Gallery, 1976, pp. 35-57, 73-99. Black & white illustrations.

M

Millett, Clair A. *A collection of dancers, meanings, symbolisms and colors from the artists notes on Hopi & Zuni kachina dancers coloring book.* Phoenix, AZ: Emby Originals, 1973. Unnumbered. Black & white illustrations.

Mills, George. *Kachinas and saints, a contrast in style and culture.* Colorado Springs: Colorado Springs Fine Arts Center, 1953 ?. Unnumbered. Black & white and color illustrations.

Minor, Marz, and Minor, Nono. *The American Indian craft book.* Lincoln and London: University of Nebraska Press © 1972, pp. 143, 145-148. Black & white illustrations.

Museum of New Mexico. Laboratory of Anthropology. *Nathaniel Owings' kachina collection.* 1973, 11 pp. Black & white illustrations.

Museum of Northern Arizona. *An introduction to Hopi kachinas.* Flagstaff: © 1977, 24pp. Published with the Arizona Bank in conjunction with an exhibition of kachinas from the collections of the Museum of Northern Arizona. Black & white and color illustrations; also front cover.

N

Naylor, Maria, ed. *Authentic Indian design.* New York: Dover, 1975, pp. 201, 204-207. Black & white illustrations. 2500 illustrations from Bureau of American Ethnology reports.

Nequatewa, Edmund. "Chaveyo: the first kachina." *Plateau,* 20:4 April 1948, pp. 60-62.

The New Encyclopaedia Britannica. Macropaedia. Chicago: © 1976, vol. 1, pp. 660, 679-80. Color illustrations.

The New Encyclopaedia Britannica. Micropaedia. Chicago: © 1976, vol. 5, p. 653. Color illustrations.

O

Oglesby, Catharine. *Modern primitive arts of Mexico, Guatemala and the Southwest.* New York: Whittlesey House, © 1939, pp. 62-66.

O'Kane, Walter C. *Sun in the sky.* Norman, OK: University of Oklahoma Press, 1950, pp. 183-192. Black & white and illustrations; illustration on p. 34.

Otis, Raymond. *Indian art of the Southwest.* Santa Fe: Southwest Indian Fair, 1931, p. 25.

R

Rogers, Faith. "Kachina dolls; Indian dolls." *Creative Crafts,* 6 Aug. 1979, pp. 62-63. Illustrated.

S

Santa Fean. "Kachinas, figurines neither toys nor idols." 1:6, August 1973, pp. 7-9. Black & white illustrations.

School Arts Magazine. "Hopi ceremonial dolls." 28:10, June 1929, p. 619. Black & white illustrations.

Sides, Dorothy S. *Decorative art of the Southwestern Indians.* New York: Dover, 1961. Black & white illustrations (Plate 18).

Simons, Carol. "Kachinas and the Hopi world." *Smithsonian Magazine,* 12:8, November 1981, p. 263. Color illustrations.

Singer, Opal Edna. "Abbot Sakiestewa, Hopi doll maker." *Arizona Highways,* 31, August 1955, p. 4-7.

Smith, Mrs. White Mountain. "Hopi gods in masquerade." *Desert,* 3:4, February 1940, pp. 19-21. Black & white illustrations.

Stribling, Mary Lou. *Crafts from North American Indian arts; techniques, designs and contemporary applications.* New York: Crown, © 1975, p. 16. Black & white illustrations.

Stuart, Jozefa, and Ashton, Robert, Jr. *Images of American Indian Art.* New York: Walker, 1977, pp. 5, 26, 30-31. Black & white and color illustrations.

Swift, Ted. "The katcina doll." *School Arts Magazine,* 30:7, March 1931, pp. 446-448. Black & white illustrations.

Sunset. "Hopi kachinas throng to California." 164, June 1980, pp. 92-93. Illustrations.

Sunset. "Meet the kachinas." 140, Feb. 1968, pp. 58-63. Illustrations.

SOWI-ING
Deer kachina. Animals are believed to assist the Hopi in curing disease and overcoming dangers.

T

Tanner, Clara L. *Ray Manley's Hopi kachinas.* Tucson, AZ: Ray Manley Photography, Inc., not dated, 32 pp. Color illustrations; front & back covers.

_____. *Southwest Indian craft arts.* Tucson: University of Arizona, © 1968, 1975, pp. 151-163. Black & white and color illustrations.

Tanner, John F. "Hopi kachinas." *Ray Manley's Collecting Southwestern Indian arts & crafts.* Tucson: Ray Manley Photography, Inc., not dated, pp. 12-16. Color illustrations.

V

Vaillant, George C. *Indian arts in North America.* New York: Harper, 1939, plates 40-43. Black & white illustrations.

Voth, H.R. *Hopi material culture.* Flagstaff, AZ: Heard Museum and Northland Press, 1978, 224 pp. Black & white illustrations.

W

Washburn, Dorothy K., ed. *Hopi kachina, spirit of life.* California Academy of Sciences, 1980, 158 pp. Black & white and color illustrations.

Waters, Frank. *Book of the Hopi.* New York: Ballantine Books, © 1963, 423 pp. A basic book for understanding the Hopi religious views and the role of the kachinas in Indian life and ceremony.

KOYEMSI

*Mudhead, another of the clown figures whose function is divided
between amusing the audience and presenting object lessons or
social commentary.*

White, Leslie A. *Zia — the sun symbol pueblo.* Albuquerque, NM: The University of Albuquerque in collaboration with Calvin Horn Publisher, Inc., 1974, pp. 236-250. A reprint of the Smithsonian Institution Bureau of American Ethnology Bulletin 184, *The Pueblo of Sia, New Mexico,* Washington: U.S. Gov't Print. Off., 1962. Black & white illustrations; plates 8 & 9.

Whiteford, Andrew H. *North American Indian arts.* New York: Golden Press, © 1970, p. 101. Color illustration.

Wright, Barton. *Hopi kachinas; the complete guide to collecting kachina dolls.* Flagstaff, AZ: Northland Press, © 1977, 139 pp. Color illustrations.

_____. *Kachinas, a Hopi artist's documentary.* Phoenix, AZ: Heard Museum, Northland Press, 1973, 272 pp. Original paintings by Cliff Bahnimptewa. Color illustrations.

_____. *Kachinas, the Barry Goldwater collection at the Heard Museum.* Phoenix, AZ: Heard Museum, W.A. Krueger, 1975, 60 pp. Color illustrations.

_____. "Kachinas." *Arizona Highways Indian arts and crafts,* Clara L. Tanner, ed. Phoenix, AZ: *Arizona Highways,* © 1976, pp. 68-99. Color illustrations.

Wright, Barton, and Roat, Evelyn. *This is a Hopi kachina.* Flagstaff, AZ: Northern Arizona Society of Science and Art, 1962, 28pp. Black & white illustrations. color front cover.

_____, and _____. _____. Rev. ed. Flagstaff, AZ: Museum of Northern Arizona, © 1975, 28 pp. Black & white and color illustrations.

NOTES

NOTES